KAISHA MCCREA

Unlocking Your Leadership

Achieve Success and Change Organizations!

Contents

Introduction

Welcome to *Unlocking Your Leadership, Achieve Success and Change Organizations!* I am Kaisha McCrea, CEO & Founder of Growing Perspectives Career Consulting. I started the Women in Leadership community as an initiative of Growing Perspectives Career Consulting , which helps professionals grow and thrive in their careers and as leaders through career coaching, leadership coaching, executive coaching, and customized team training. I wanted to start a firm that can support people in their desire to be as successful as possible, regardless of where they are in their career.

My desire with the community was to create a space where women leaders could connect, share, support and celebrate each other. Our community started in 2021 as a Facebook group, Women that Lead, that has grown over the years and has led to the first book of our Women in Leadership initiative, *Unlocking Your Leadership, Achieve Success and Change Organizations!*. This book is co-authored with two previous guest speakers at our Women in Leadership breakfasts. I am thankful to have Jana Pollard and Bernadette Spencer join me to continue supporting the success of women leaders.

Women leaders are everywhere. We can lead in any role with the right resources, knowledge, influence and support. I want to encourage any woman doubting their ability to lead to enjoy the enclosed stories. My desire for any woman leader that needs encouragement to continue their growth and success is to leverage the lessons and examples shared in this book.

My career has not been a straight path. My decisions have not always perfectly aligned with my career or leadership aspirations. There were times where I was extremely confident and proactive with my career and there were times when I did not step forward to pursue opportunities due to fear or doubt.

I know how it feels to let a good opportunity pass and I also know the joy and excitement of seizing opportunities to grow and have greater impact as a leader in my community, company, and business. I have had the opportunity and time to reflect on my career, which has revealed an increased awareness and understanding of my leadership strengths as well as areas I need to focus on to continue my growth and success. I now make more intentional decisions of where and how I spend my time and invest in my professional development to ensure alignment with my leadership aspirations and goals.

We each have a choice to determine our path when opportunities are presented or when we discover opportunities. My hope is that this book will prepare you to pursue opportunities that support your success as a leader to change organizations.

The words in this book are a combination of over 60 years of experience between three successful women leaders. Each author wrote different chapters enclosed in this book. Our names are shown following each chapter. A quick summary of our chapters are enclosed below for ease and quick reference when needed. I wrote the first three chapters. Chapters 4 and 5 are written by Jana Pollard. Chapters 6 and 8 are written by me. Chapter 7 is written by Bernadette Spencer.

Chapter 1 - Why Not You?

You can excel at the level you desire as a leader within your current role, outside of your role, and in your future. Why not you?

I will highlight a few areas that impacted my leadership that once addressed allowed me to become more successful and impactful in any organization. I hope these insights will support you in further Unlocking your Leadership. In the next three chapters we will explore fear, perfectionism and opportunities.

I experienced a great career of over 20 years in Corporate America with a Fortune 500 company. My corporate career started in engineering and expanded to roles in sales, consulting, operations and supply chain. I had the opportunity to lead teams as a team manager, project manager, continuous improvement consultant and other operations roles. I worked across several businesses and in different assignments in my corporate career. Some of these different assignments required moving to a different group, business , industry or state. There were times I only knew a few people in the new assignment. I had to learn new processes, products, cultures and businesses. As a small business owner I have leveraged my corporate experiences, skill set, relationships and knowledge as I continue growing as a leader and entrepreneur.

I remember a question that a colleague asked when I was about 10 years into my career - "What are you good at?" This colleague and I recently started working together and it was a way for them to understand my core competencies or key areas of expertise. I appreciated this inquiry from my colleague and felt that it was a way to further understand and share our backgrounds, experience and expertise.

This question though brief and without much additional detail, caused me to think further about my top strengths & attributes. I held several roles in my career that allowed me to further understand the main areas I excelled in and where my key strengths can have the most impact in organizations and groups. Those strengths revolve around a desire to learn, a high level of business acumen and understanding, adapting to different situations, and being a problem solver. These strengths were developed from my engineering background and unique career experiences in various businesses and roles within my career.

I have worked with several women leaders and professionals in my role as a Career & Leadership Coach. On occasions, I've reminded them of their expertise, experience and encouraged them to further recognize these.

"You don't have to be great to start, but you have to start to be great." Zig Ziglar

Earlier in my career within the manufacturing industry, I remember a high-level manager describing my work ethic as one of a "can do" attitude.

At that time, I was a young engineer who was eager to try new opportunities. I was not afraid of change or learning new concepts, processes, or cultures. I often had an optimistic mindset when opportunities or challenges were presented, especially when managing projects, considering new approaches or options for process improvements.

In roles where I was an individual contributor, where I had no employees reporting to me, I had to lead through influence. As a contract administrator, I utilized metrics to foster collaboration between the company I worked for and manufacturing vendors across the US. This resulted in improved business performance, vendor reliability and quality results. In sales, influence is the name of the game. That was a role where establishing and maintaining trust were crucial to the customer relationship. That trust was not only built on the products and services I sold, but also on ensuring excellent results, managing the expectations and needs of the customer along with those of my employer.

Later in my career, a manager acknowledged my level of flexibility in the way I approached my work, and this distinguished me from my peers and helped me excel. I was a consultant working across the corporation in a new work group and by this point, I had worked in manufacturing, sales, and continuous improvement roles. These roles instilled a level of flexibility and deepened my understanding of businesses, processes and products that proved beneficial.

As a corporate consultant, I was willing to learn new approaches, adapt quickly to new cultures and leverage best practices. Rapidly adjust to new initiatives, challenges and opportunities. Quickly incorporate feedback and changes to meet the objectives of the organizations and clients I supported. I gained a more complete view of the corporation & practices within several businesses. This experience was priceless as it allowed a high level of autonomy, creativity and impact. Being agile before it became a project management methodology.

Reflect on what are your top strengths or skills.

What have others told you about your top skills and strengths?

What do you think your top skills and strengths are?

What skills or strengths do you want to develop further ?

What skills or strengths do you want to use more?

Starting where you are !

Women-owned businesses continue to fuel the economy, representing nearly 40 percent of all businesses (over 14 million), employing 12.2 million workers, and generating $2.7 trillion in revenue, according to the 2024 Wells Fargo Impact of Women-Owned Business Report.

In addition, the number of new woman-owned businesses continue to grow, expanding at nearly double the rate of those owned by men – increasing by 4.5 times from 2022 to 2023, according to a 2024 article by Wells Fargo & Company: "New Report Finds Growth of Woman Business Owners Outpaces the Market."

I thought it was helpful to remind us of the significant impact women business owners have on our economy. This is a reminder of what is possible as women leaders and business owners. There is an abundance of opportunities available to us. My impact as a woman business owner is helping businesses, organizations, and individuals thrive, and support my community by helping people see and further achieve what is possible in their careers and as leaders. Being active in the Chesterfield Chamber of Commerce and other organizations have allowed me to further understand what's happening in the community and identify ways I can contribute. I gained additional leadership experience by serving in distinct roles within the chamber of commerce, including currently serving on the Board of Directors and previously as the Chair of its DE&I Committee. I will begin my tenure as the Chair of the Board of Directors during this year.

These professional opportunities did not fall into my lap. Nor did I feel the pressure of having a certain amount of success before going after these opportunities. Do not wait until you feel everything is perfect. Opportunities may only come around once, so strongly consider each opportunity and be willing to take calculated risks to pursue your goals as a leader. Leadership requires a certain amount of courage to pursue opportunities others may not fully support.

I remember a few times during my career when I lacked support while pursuing new areas or roles outside my typical degree or experience path. I overcame those moments of resistance through the help of my network and key supporters along with delivering excellent work, being persistent, and communicating my value to others in and across my organization. In future chapters we will discuss the need to understand and communicate your value in your organization and the power of our networks.

This lack of support can also come from within. Earlier in my career, there were times when I questioned my abilities. I questioned if I could be successful in certain roles and ended up not pursuing them. I thought I needed to be an expert at times before pursuing those opportunities. It wasn't until later in my career that I noticed how confident some colleagues sounded and appeared with much less experience and sometimes less expertise. They did not wait until they had an extensive background in that area before volunteering or accepting the next opportunity.

This hesitation came from an element of perfectionism and a fear of failure. I can say I have experienced on a couple of occasions a fear of success. I didn't even realize that it was possible to have a fear of success until I heard a local speaker share insights on this topic. For someone who has led teams and initiatives, this came as a shock. Overcoming this fear of success involved taking time to reflect on what I truly valued and desired in my career, and what I had worked so hard for and the future I envisioned for myself. I also observed other successful people that I admired and noticed how they effectively managed their success and relationships as they rose in their career. This helped me to move past this fear of success. I continued to increase my knowledge, impact and visibility, from attending conferences to utilizing different resources – i.e., mentors and books. Now I can better recognize when these fears are present and can quickly implement behaviors to quickly move forward.

Being able to overcome fears and adapt effectively are valuable and necessary skills for my success and growth as a dynamic leader. It allowed me to quickly learn how to impact organizations, form relationships, and build trust with those I supported and led. As I have grown and evolved as a leader the value of communicating my progress and results has been a key building block of my success. I value keeping everyone informed and documenting progress of key efforts, projects, and decisions. Communication is a key element of my leadership style and a way to keep others involved and connected. This has truly benefited my career, especially as a small business owner.

What fears have you experienced or are you experiencing as a leader or in your career?

What fears do you need to address?

How are your fears impacting your success or growth?

How do you plan to address your fears?

What opportunities do you desire to pursue next in your career?

What will it take for you to move forward?

What opportunities have you passed on?

How can you identify similar opportunities in the future?

What will you do differently?

Next Steps:

UNLOCKING YOUR LEADERSHIP

Goals for Chapter 1

What goals would you like to set for yourself based on this chapter?

Are there areas where you are facing resistance as a leader?

How would like to address these areas?

Author: Kaisha McCrea, MBA

Chapter 2 - Believing in Yourself

You have to believe that you can be successful as a leader. I am a firm believer that we all can be successful in our careers with the right resources, support, skills, and experiences. As women leaders, we have to continue to "believe what our resumes say about us". I shared this statement during a women's summit hosted recently by the Richmond Metropolitan Business League. It reminds us of the importance to further believe in our demonstrated results, impact and experiences as we continue in our careers and consider leadership or growth opportunities. This belief and confidence is essential for our success and development.

Early in my career a more experienced colleague shared this with me: "Don't get intimidated if you don't know something. You can learn it."

This brief statement gave me courage and confidence that regardless of any challenges or doubts I had during this job assignment, I could address it. This was a reminder to not become frustrated or shrink if I had challenges and to remember that I can continue to learn and grow.

13

It also contributed to my development of having a growth mindset, which is key to have as a leader. A growth mindset is one where you believe there are possibilities. It's understanding that certain outcomes, potential or people are not fixed, that we can still grow, we can still develop, and we still have options. You can refer to the book "The Growth Mindset" by Carol Dweck for more insights on this approach.

I embrace the belief that I can still evolve, adapt and change during my career. It looks like getting multiple certifications after 15 years in Corporate America. I particularly remember being one of two of the oldest people in a "fast track" training program for Supply Chain and being able to carve out the time needed to complete my certification courses and exams successfully. I remember obtaining my International Coaching Federation certification training and assessment after leaving Corporate America. That's what the growth mindset is. It allows me to take bold moves and venture into new areas for growth in my business. I will continue pursuing ways to continue to grow as a leader.

It encourages me to continue to learn and extend my expertise in different areas. It's being willing to transition to a new business or organization with your existing skill sets and leveraging your knowledge to make an impact in these opportunities while continuing to learn new approaches and businesses. It is being willing to move to a different state, adjusting to new cultures and processes for career advancement opportunities. I had the confidence and belief in my abilities that allowed me to say - "Yes, I'm capable of doing this." and pursue challenging, diverse and desired opportunities during my career.

I fully embrace the growth mindset because it strengthens our abilities to continue learning and growing in our careers as leaders. We are not fixed in our growth potential or the knowledge we can obtain. We can continue to learn. We can change and thrive!

Where do you need to further develop as a leader?

What areas as a leader have been most challenging for you?

What are your aspirations as a leader?

Value Your Experience and Potential

It may not come naturally for everyone to acknowledge and share their value and experiences with others. There is a misconception that others will always recognize our abilities. There is also a misconception that there is something wrong with sharing your expertise or accomplishments with others. It is necessary to self-promote and share your skills and abilities as we are all very busy. It is not always possible for others to be aware of the work that you do as a leader, be aware of your impact or accomplishments.

"People who are good at promoting themselves tend to have a higher profile in their industry and a stronger network," according to the Guide to Becoming More Confident at Self-

Promotion from Indeed Career Guide.

These people are generally confident in sharing their strengths and personal brands and understand their value in the market as employees, partners or entrepreneurs, according to the guide, which added that promoting yourself helps you "become a better leader as you use your skills to mentor others and to promote your team."

If you're new to self-promotion, here are a few helpful ways to share your accomplishments:

- Utilize social media to highlight key awards, progress or achievements. You can share with key mentors, supporters, friends, and family.
- Share your accomplishments in a newsletter (create your own if needed), newspaper articles or blogs.
- Highlight your accomplishments in your bio, resume, and LinkedIn profile.

Earlier in my career, a business leader advised that I send quarterly newsletters with updates on my key activities to the entire department. This made quite a difference for me as a newer employee by raising my visibility within the organization and sharing broadly my accomplishments and initiatives . This allowed my colleagues and leaders at various levels across the business to become more aware of the scope and depth of my work and skills. This action created opportunities for my colleagues to further inquire about my results and helped open the doors for expanded opportunities and increased responsibilities in that role. I moved from that position to a more customer facing role that allowed me to directly manage larger revenue clients for our business with more responsibility and exposure.

Sharing your experiences not only highlights your potential but allows others to be aware of your skills, interests, growth, and impact. This can help lead to other opportunities and increase awareness of you and your skills.

Where do you need to further advocate or share your accomplishments, potential and recognition?

Who are others that can support you to further promote and share your achievements?

Who else should know about your growth and progress?

Supporting your Leadership Skills

We each have talents and skills that create our unique leadership styles.

There are numerous opportunities to develop and display your leadership skills at your job and in your community.

During my corporate career, I volunteered to lead and co-lead several different organizations or participated in a leadership capacity in different groups, including my employer's Women Employee Resource Group that I served in for several years. This opportunity allowed me to interface with senior leaders, create strategies, and work in a leadership capacity with other professionals across the company. This gave me the opportunity to attend conferences and gain experience that supported my growth as a leader.

I had another opportunity to serve on the board of directors of a professional chapter for Supply Chain professionals. This allowed me to continue developing my leadership skills and connect with colleagues in other companies.

I currently serve on the board of directors for the Chester-field Chamber of Commerce. This allows me to work with other leaders and support the leadership of the local chamber, including programming, financial, and strategic efforts, as well as growing and identifying key initiatives that support business communities and professionals. Being a part of my local chamber of commerce has provided increased visibility of my business, networking opportunities with other businesses and professionals to support my professional and business' growth.

There is a wealth of opportunities available to support your growth as a leader. Not every opportunity may appear relevant at the moment but being strategic and intentional will allow you to identify key opportunities that can support your needs to grow further as a leader.

Identify one or two organizations or groups that you can contact to identify opportunities for leadership roles.

What opportunities would you like to pursue to further develop your leadership skills?

Managing your Brand as a Leader!

It is very important to be aware of your image and brand as a leader, which involves reflecting and considering what you are best known for or what you're best at. How would you like to be remembered as a leader?

Our reputation as leaders is priceless and greatly impacts our growth potential and advancement. Karen Gulliford, executive coach and founder of Great Workplaces LLC, said it best: **"Networking is no good without a good reputation and expertise. You have to be good at your career or profession."**

Good reputation, among other things, can come as a byproduct of good results. Your reputation will lead to door of opportunities for your growth and success. In my corporate consultant role, I worked across the corporation and was exposed to change management , coaching and leadership development. The impact of meeting and exceeding my business client objectives and requirements with improved processes, metrics and approaches resulted in opportunities to continue to grow and expand my level of responsibilities. I maximized my time in this role to learn change management from more experienced colleagues. Once I had a deeper level of expertise, I was offered the opportunity to develop and provide training in change management and leadership development within my group. I developed a change management certification program for our global consultant team which allowed our team to provide similar approaches and resources for our business clients.

This experience and the recognition for managing and implementing this program, allowed me a chance to work with other change management professionals across the corporation. I was able to provide training for specific groups including supply chain and customer service teams in various businesses. This was an example of how my reputation, expertise and proven results continued to open additional doors of leadership and growth. Another example is when I was in contract operations, where I collaborated with several key suppliers to turn around or further improve their business performance. These results further established a reputation that allowed me to work on other key projects and led to a promotion to a global supply chain improvement position.

Deliver with Excellence

How well do you deliver results?

Do you deliver results with excellence? Do you meet or exceed expectations? Are you proactive with your leadership approach? Are you leaving an impact with your results?

Thinking through these questions will help you assess how well you are providing value to your organization, team, or business. If any improvement is needed, do not hesitate to address these areas and determine if additional support or resources are needed.

"You have to be good - you have to work hard at your craft. Stay in touch with the latest trends. And be relevant," Karen Gulliford, executive coach and founder of Great Workplaces LLC.

Learn from Your Experiences

"I never lose. I either win or learn," Nelson Mandela.

Every experience is a learning opportunity. We have limited time in each role so we want to maximize our chances of growth and success as leaders by leveraging knowledge and expertise gained in current and former positions.

Asking for Help or Support

As leaders, we may believe that we need to know all the answers or do everything on our own. The reality is that we can benefit from help. Do not be afraid to ask for help when you are faced with challenges as a leader or when you are trying to develop a new skill. We all may need help or support when encountering new opportunities, challenges, or areas of growth that are outside our current skill set. Seeking support has several benefits. It can provide additional insight, clarity and resources to accelerate and strengthen your decisions and improved results.

Earlier in my career, I felt the need to know everything or be able to do everything. This was not realistic, and it caused unnecessary self-pressure. Realize that there are various levels of expectations placed on you based on your role and responsibilities. Try to limit the amount of unnecessary self-imposed and unrealistic expectations that can negatively impact your performance. Seek feedback from mentors, advisors, managers, coaches, and others to discuss expectations for alignment, clarity or further understanding. Utilize this feedback to adjust or align with realistic expectations and goals for yourself and development.

Next Steps:

UNLOCKING YOUR LEADERSHIP

Goals for Chapter 2

What goals would you like to set for yourself based on this chapter?

Author: Kaisha McCrea, MBA

Chapter 3 - Power in Networks & Mentors

Networking is essential in our careers as leaders. It can provide greater access to resources, opportunities, and information. Networking involves relationship building and can increase awareness of ourselves, situations, and environments. Building a strong network of supporters and advisors is key to our growth, development, and success. I still have mentors supporting me as I continue to grow as a leader. I have also mentored others on their leadership journey. Leadership is not an individual sport. We may have individual results and responsibilities, but we often rely on the contributions of others to support our goals and aspirations. We can benefit from the support and insight of others as we grow as leaders.

I had one mentor whose feedback was beneficial at a key moment in my career. He shared that my manager thought I was a perfectionist, which caused me to complete some assignments at a slower pace, but once I completed an assignment I would "blow it out of the water"! This feedback helped me understand how I was perceived by others and the limitations I unnecessarily placed on myself that impacted performance.

After receiving this feedback, I was intentional about taking more risks, utilizing additional resources, and seeking colleague feedback. If my mentor had not shared his thoughts with me, I may not have fully grasped the need to change. This resulted in an excellent experience in that role, which expanded my responsibilities and resulted in a promotion to a new role.

We must be willing to receive feedback from our managers, trusted advisors, mentors, and sponsors as we grow as leaders. Not all feedback will be positive, but it will present you with opportunities to make adjustments and move forward to excel as leaders.

But there is a balance in the type of feedback you solicit from your circle of supporters. I made a conscious decision to distance myself from a colleague that I felt was not adding to my growth process based on the negative questioning related to my new career path. I would advise you to assess how colleagues, mentors, managers or supporters are aligned with your long-term vision and connect with those most aligned with your vision and who understand your potential and skills.

I realized later in my career that not everyone is comfortable with receiving positive performance feedback. I caution you from being too modest or humble to accept and document the positive feedback you receive from your managers and others. This type of recognition is beneficial as you consider different roles and advancement.

Who are some of your role models or mentors in leadership that you connect with?

Where would you like to grow further as a leader?

Your Group of Supporters & Support System

When I left corporate after 20+ years, one of the first people I contacted was my colleague, Jana Pollard. I wanted to contact my core group of leaders, supporters, colleagues, and family regarding this change in my life. Jana was one of the initial people I shared this update with because we knew each other for over 15 years and we held each other in high professional regard. It is a great honor to co-author this book with her.

Who you let into your inner circle makes a difference in your career, growth, and success. Who is in your circle today? Who supports you as a leader? Who can you depend on when you face challenges? Choose your circle very wisely as you may need to lean on it during your career.

Who is in your circle of supporters today?

What changes should you make to your current circle?

Are there any roles missing? If so, which are missing and how would you like to address this missing role?

Networking Tips

**"When you think of networking you can't do just one thing,"
said Karen Gulliford, executive coach and founder of Great
Workplaces LLC.** "If you focus on one piece of networking you
might miss the other opportunities and you miss the chance to
meet new people. Vary how you network so you don't saturate
where you are."

When speaking with Karen, she advised that we should consider
large and small groups as well as one-on-one of networking.
Either way, there is an element of intentionality that is required
to build, maintain, and grow your network. Networking can look
different for each of us. A few examples can be committees at
your work, in your community or school. Business groups, char-
itable organizations and work events are other opportunities to
network. You can also share updates with colleagues or a simple
text or phone call to stay in touch. These are all ways to begin
networking.

There is value in being intentional at maintaining your networks
and staying connected with your core supporters, mentors, and
advisors. I had one mentor share with me that "it's easier to
stay in touch than to reintroduce yourself to someone if you
haven't stayed in touch with them." A few ways to maintain
connection with your key connections is to understand how they
prefer to stay in touch and communicate with them through
those channels. I remember setting reminders on my calendar
to contact specific colleagues , which I still do.

How well are you maintaining your network?

What areas of improvement have you identified?

Where are you excelling as it relates to networking?

Next Steps:

UNLOCKING YOUR LEADERSHIP

Goals for Chapter 3

What goals would you like to set for yourself based on this chapter?

Author–Kaisha McCrea, MBA (CEO & Founder of Growing Perspectives®)

Jana Pollard will share with us in the next two chapters insights and tips on the power we have as women leaders and why our decisions matter.

Chapter 4 - You Have the Power

In a world where external influences and conformity are on the rise, it's essential to form personal opinions and express them openly. It's important to express your opinion because you want to be authentic in how you portray yourself. This makes it a lot easier to be a leader because you're being you.

Plus, it's too much to keep up with being fake and phony because you must continue putting up a certain persona. It's important to be authentic because you don't even have to think about it, right? Be the leader you know you can be and get things done.

For example, a lot of my friends and family know that I do not like bugs. You must keep things tidy, which helps prevent pest issues. I replicated this mindset in the workplace as a manufacturing leader where one of my plants was not being maintained properly resulting in visible bugs. I instituted regular exterminations and cleaning standards, which created a culture of cleanliness that was noticed by our customers and appreciated by the employees. By being authentic, I was able to leverage my personal standards in the workplace to make it a better place.

Trusting in oneself means having confidence in decisions, worth, and abilities. A 2019 LinkedIn Gender Insights Report found that women are 14% less likely than men to apply for a job after viewing it. Women need self-trust to make confident decisions, knowing they possess the inner strength to succeed.

My manager recommended that I apply for a maintenance supervisor role. But after a few years as an engineer, this created a crossroads. I was always passionate about problem-solving and innovation, but there was a calling to expand my horizons and embrace new challenges.

I thought I wasn't going to get the job. I went to school for engineering, and I thought that was going to be my career. But after thinking about her recommendation and the opportunity to have more of an impact as a leader than an individual contributor, I applied for and got the job. The shift was both exciting and daunting. My engineering background provided a foundation in technical knowledge and analytical thinking, but managing operations required different skills. Taking the initiative to learn about supply chain management, process optimization, and team leadership involved formal education, on-the-job learning, and mentorship from experienced colleagues.

As an operations manager, my responsibilities included overseeing daily operations, ensuring efficiency, and managing a diverse team. This experience underscored the importance of effective communication, strategic planning, and the ability to adapt to changing circumstances. Problems were viewed from a broader perspective, considering not just technical aspects but also human and business factors.

After several successful years managing operations, my confidence grew in addressing challenging situations, including an underperforming plant. Believing that strong leadership and strategic direction was needed, I set out to take on the challenge of leading this underperforming manufacturing site.

Before approaching leadership with the premonition, I completed a thorough analysis of the facility's performance and identified key improvement areas. This prework resulted in the creation of a strategic plan for the facility. After sharing this plan with senior leaders, I was offered the opportunity.

Engaging with employees, communicating the vision, and fostering a culture of collaboration and continuous improvement became top priorities in this new role. The turnaround wasn't instantaneous, but progress was evident over time. The facility did not have enough room to grow so it was decided to leverage owned assets by expanding into an existing facility rather than leasing a new facility. This allowed for resource optimization and greater operational control. Operational efficiency improved, production targets were met, and employee morale soared. Positive customer feedback returned, and the facility's reputation as a top performer was restored.

Reflecting on this experience emphasizes the value of self-trust and the courage to step up when opportunities arise. Believing in my abilities and presenting a clear vision made it possible to lead the facility to success and make a lasting impact on the organization. I didn't care about the personal visibility, I loved the challenge of solving problems. You have the power to create the life you want.

"One of the most fascinating consistencies in research about men, women, and communication is the finding that as women, we have a tendency to underestimate our own potential," said Valorie Burton in her book, *Successful Women Speak Differently – 9 Habits that build Confidence, Courage, and Influence.*

Let's change that narrative. We have the potential to do whatever it is we set our mind, body, and hearts to by getting out of our own way. Women can sometimes hesitate to assert themselves, trust others over their own instincts or not realize the extent of their power . This must change starting now! Whether it's applying for jobs, navigating professional relationships, or dealing with personal situations, we must remember that we don't have to meet every condition perfectly. We can take risks, trust ourselves, and assert our worth.

Unlocking your leadership starts with self-belief, courage, and the willingness to embrace challenges — even when they seem daunting. Embracing your personal journey means recognizing that your inner strength can turn setbacks into steppingstones. Every decision made and every step forward, even when imperfect, is an act of claiming one's power. As women, we often face societal pressures and expectations, but we can also break through them by building confidence, speaking up, and taking action.

By unlocking our leadership, we not only redefine our paths but also pave the way for others to do the same. Each of us has the power to lead by example, to advocate for ourselves, and inspire others to do the same.

Chapter Exercise:

Describe a specific career aspiration, personal goal, or dream.

List the actions needed to achieve the above aspiration, goal, or aspiration. Include an expected date to complete each action.

1. _____
2. _____
3. _____
4. _____
5. _____

Next Steps:

UNLOCKING YOUR LEADERSHIP

What goals would you like to set for yourself based on this chapter?

Author : Jana Pollard, MBA

Chapter 5- Your Decisions Matter

"Listen to the inner voice that encourages you. Shut out the one that discourages you." – Cathy Guisewite

Your inner positive voice is empowering. It encourages, motivates, and gives you the positive push you need to pursue your goals and overcome challenges. However, there is another inner voice that can discourage you. Do not let this negative voice influence your actions and dominate you. By intentionally choosing to listen to the encouraging voice, you develop the mindset to take risks, try new things, and reach your full potential.

Which voice would you rather listen to? After all, we all act upon what we hear. And we are our own biggest influencer.

My own journey is a testament to the profound ripple effects of listening to one's positive voice. Born and raised in Brooklyn, New York, I made the bold decision to venture beyond the city limits and pursue higher education at North Carolina A&T State University. Despite knowing the field of mechanical engineering was male-dominated, I refused to let that deter me. I was determined to carve out my own path, knowing the challenges ahead would sharpen my resolve.

That resolve was challenged when with one semester left before graduation, I became pregnant. The news sent shockwaves through my carefully laid plans, leaving me torn between the competing demands of motherhood and career aspirations.

Despite the uncertainty and upheaval, I made the courageous decision to stay the course and complete my education. I juggled morning sickness, classes, and job interviews. With unwavering determination and the support of my loved ones, I persevered, graduating with honors and earning a Bachelor of Science in Mechanical Engineering.

Juggling these major responsibilities early in life gave me the confidence to conquer anything. In a serendipitous twist of fate, the company that extended a job offer prior to graduation relocated me to New Jersey, allowing me to be closer to family during this pivotal time in my life. The birth of my first child brought an abundance of joy and blessings, and I was deeply touched by the outpouring of love and support from my coworkers, who threw me a surprise baby shower.

Reflecting on this chapter of my life, I am reminded of the inherent power that resides within each of us—the power to navigate life's twists and turns with courage, resilience, and grace. Merriam-Webster defines power as the "ability to act or produce an effect," and indeed, my journey is a testament to the transformative power of choice.

Managing Your Stress

According to the American Psychological Association, women experience higher stress levels compared to men, with nearly 60% of women in the U.S. reporting daily stress versus 48% of men. This increased stress often stems from balancing multiple roles and responsibilities, both personally and professionally – which makes complete sense.

Women take care of themselves and others. And it can be a lot to manage. We don't show it because we can internalize things to the point that we don't ask for help, so we end up absorbing the stress instead of trying to alleviate it.

We must prioritize taking care of ourselves. I was inspired when I heard Sheila Battle, a visionary of The 15 Minutes of Grace philosophy, talk about her philosophy at a Junior League meeting. It's pretty simple (in theory) and straightforward. Take 15 minutes a day to sit in silence. At first it was difficult to carve out 15 minutes but when I did I felt refreshed and stress free. Do whatever helps you manage your stress effectively so that you're refreshed and able to take on the next challenge.

Because guess what? Those boulders aren't moving, and your kids will still be there. They will need you. Your career will be there as well. If you continue to pay it the attention it needs. You need to find that outlet to relieve your stress. Don't let those boulders topple you.

To effectively manage and mitigate stress at work, I found that employing strategies such as careful listening and remaining calm are crucial. These approaches not only help me maintain my well-being but also enable me to make more thoughtful and effective decisions.

In decision-making, the value of diverse perspectives is indispensable. Women bring unique insights and experiences that often lead to more inclusive and effective solutions, particularly in complex situations. This was evident during a critical operational challenge at a manufacturing site I managed.

We needed to mobilize resources from a nearby facility and the most qualified candidates were a group of women operators who excelled at our main site. However, these women were uncomfortable with driving on the highway to train others at the new facility.

What initially appeared to be a minor logistical issue quickly escalated into a major point of contention. My male counterparts, focused solely on operational needs, proposed a harsh solution: Threatening to fire the employees if they did not comply. While their approach was direct and aimed at meeting operational goals, it disregarded the human element. Recognizing that the women's discomfort was a genuine concern and not a matter of defiance, I opted for a more empathetic and practical approach.

Perceptions can often shape how decisions are received. In this case, threatening the employees could have reinforced negative stereotypes and led to further resentment. Instead, by making the decision to arrange transportation, I demonstrated a commitment to creating a supportive and respectful work environment. This decision not only resolved the logistical issue but also highlighted the importance of addressing perceived concerns and maintaining positive relationships with employees. By alleviating their stress and validating their concerns, we fostered a sense of appreciation and loyalty.

The impact of this approach was substantial. With transportation in place, productivity at the new facility surged. The women, feeling valued and supported, performed their duties with excellence and quickly helped other employees get up to speed. This not only increased overall efficiency but also underscored the effectiveness of considering both operational goals and employee well-being.

Integrating principles such as careful listening, remaining calm, and understanding who to involve has been essential in managing stress and achieving successful outcomes. These principles are critical to authenticity. In addition, flexibility and reason were critical to the success of this situation. I suggested that we try the arrangement as a pilot. I also asked my colleagues this: Why are we punishing these women who want to do the job?

I empathized with these women because I thought of my mother and sister, both of whom do not drive. They tried getting drivers licenses but were overcome by the anxiety of being on the road.

Women often bring a holistic perspective to problem-solving, balancing organizational objectives with the needs of the people involved. This approach is vital for developing sustainable solutions that benefit both the organization and its employees.

As we advocate for greater inclusion and diversity in leadership roles, it is crucial to recognize and harness the unique strengths women bring to the table. Embracing these diverse perspectives leads to more balanced and effective decision-making, driving success in ways that might not be immediately apparent to those who overlook these valuable insights. By valuing and incorporating diverse viewpoints, we address not only the operational challenges but also the perceptions and dynamics that influence workplace success, paving the way for more equitable and innovative outcomes.

My good friend Angie's experience as a supply chain leader illustrates how standing firm in your abilities and decisions can transform not only your professional path but also the perception others have of your value.

When Angie became a supply chain supervisor at a Fortune 100 technology company, she didn't expect that her main obstacles would be from fellow female leaders. As she covered for her often-absent boss, Angie's work began to get noticed. But when her boss was let go, Angie was overlooked for the position, which went to a man with no degree, no experience, and no supply chain skills. His only advantage was his familial connection to the plant manager.

Despite being sidelined, Angie remained resilient. She received major projects that should have been her male colleague's responsibility, including consolidating warehouses and overhauling the end-to-end supply chain process to improve customer experience. Angie took on the work, feeling overwhelmed at times, but determined to prove her worth. She led her team through resistance, involving production workers in key decisions and standardizing work processes. Through Angie's leadership, customer satisfaction skyrocketed from 30% to 100%.

The powerful transformation Angie spearheaded came from her belief in her ability to rise to the challenge, even when recognition didn't come from her superiors. Her story reflects the essence of a quote by Coco Chanel:

"*The most courageous act is still to think for yourself. Aloud.*"

Angie trusted herself, even in the face of adversity, and she let her results speak for themselves.

Eventually, Angie began to reflect on how this environment had shaped her. A senior leader once asked her, "Why do you always look like you're mad?" Typically a bubbly and positive person, Angie realized that she had been worn down by constantly proving herself without the corresponding acknowledgment. At that moment, Angie made a courageous decision: she left the company. It was a decision based on self-respect and the belief that she deserved better.

Angie's story shows that sometimes the hardest decisions are the most empowering. When she left her role, she placed a bet on herself. After three years at a Fortune 500 company, her previous employer came calling. They had a supply chain crisis and asked Angie what it would take for her to come back. She returned on her terms, and within a year, was promoted to the global leadership team for demand management.

Angie's story is a testament to the idea that, according to the article *Confidence Gap* by Katty Kay and Claire Shipman, ***"Success, it turns out, correlates just as closely with confidence as it does with competence."*** Angie had both, and by trusting her abilities and making bold decisions, she not only turned around challenging situations but reshaped her career trajectory.

As this chapter reflects, we, too, have the power to create the lives we want, much like Angie did. Her decision to leave a toxic environment and return only when her value was fully recognized speaks to the strength of self-trust. Her journey shows that, even when overlooked, our decisions matter. It's through trusting ourselves, having the courage to make the hard choices, and never letting doubt dictate our path that we can truly harness our power.

"You are your best thing." – *Toni Morrison*

Just like Angie, we all face moments when we must choose which voice to listen to. Let it be the voice that says *"you can."* Because you have the power to create the life you want.

What is something in your life you wish to change or shape?

Perhaps it's a career goal, a personal dream, or an aspiration that has lingered in the back of your mind. Reflect on what's holding you back. Is it time, money, or fear?

Don't let excuses stand in your way. Write a plan. Be specific about the tangible steps needed to reach your goal. Create a realistic timeline and commit to following through. Whatever the dream, know that you already possess the power to bring it to fruition. Trust yourself, because your decisions matter, and you have the strength to shape the life you envision.

Each decision you make is a step toward unlocking the leader within you. Leadership isn't just about moments when others acknowledge your abilities. It's about recognizing and acting on them yourself. Angie's journey demonstrates that standing firm in your worth and making bold choices can transform obstacles into opportunities for growth.

Your decisions shape your journey, and by embracing them with confidence and courage, you cultivate the strength to create the life and career you desire. Don't wait for permission to lead — validate yourself. Each step you take not only builds your path but strengthens the power within you.

Chapter Exercise:

- What are some moments in life when you trusted yourself and made a bold decision?How did it turn out?

- Think about a time when you doubted yourself. What was the outcome, and how might I have been different if you had trusted yourself more?

Next Steps:

UNLOCKING YOUR LEADERSHIP

Goals for Chapter 5

What goals would you like to set for yourself based on this chapter?

We will further explore ways to know your value in the next chapter. Kaisha McCrea will share additional insights with you to support identifying, communicating and leveraging your value in your organizations.

Author– Jana Pollard, MBA (Corporate Leader)

Chapter 6- Know Your Value

Know your value, articulate your value, and protect your value when you are moving through your career and growing as a leader.

Your brand, reputation, and financial well-being depend on understanding your value and how you present your value to others. It can impact every decision you make and every opportunity you pursue or decline. Regardless of what others say or do not say about your value or skill set, it is essential that we each recognize our potential, value, and importance.

When I think about the value each of us brings to organizations, it includes how we view ourselves and how others view our engagement and presence. Key objectives may differ across organizations but every group I have worked with has appreciated performance on these key areas: results, impact, collaboration, knowledge, experience, and expertise. Your performance in these key areas supports how others view your impact and value provided to organizations.

We can further identify the value we provide to organizations by understanding how our actions & results support the company's overall objectives and culture. For example, if you are recognized for achieving significant improvement initiatives for the organization or leading your team effectively through a major culture transition, this may be viewed positively by others in your organization. These are actions that are valued in your organization.

It is also essential for you to value your experience, impact, and expertise. Knowing our value does not mean we no longer need to collaborate with others or build a network of supporters, but it allows us to be a confident, powerful, and effective leader. Having this mindset allowed me to confidently walk away from an opportunity that was not aligned with my financial expectations and professional requirements.

I remember interviewing for the role a few years previously, where I was the top candidate and then being told the job was placed on hold. The same job was then reposted a few months later, but the salary range was greatly reduced. The job title may have changed but the job description was identical. When I was approached for this position, I gracefully declined the offer, knowing that the latest offer insulted my two decades of professional experience and expertise. I was disappointed by the lack of respect and assumption that I would be interested in an opportunity paying less than my skills and the work required. I was so proud of myself for not accepting less than I deserved. I chose to never engage with that corporation again following this interaction and to continue to pursue my path in entrepreneurship.

47

A few years later, I read a book, "Never Split the Difference" by Chris Voss, that helped me lean in further on walking away from deals or opportunities that are not mutually beneficial. The book included a statement that I still lean on today: "No deal is better than a bad deal."

We all have experiences, expertise, and education that are valuable in any organization. I challenge you to document and articulate your value for yourself and others. Once we fully understand our value and importance, we can confidently deliver on expectations towards our goals, including making difficult decisions to pursue our dreams and leave situations, jobs, careers or organizations that no longer serve our growth and development.

Knowing our value allows us to be come effective and confident leaders. It enables us to be able to recognize and advocate for the value of others in our organization . It also enables us to advocate more successfully for ourselves. It will allow us to pursue additional career and leadership opportunities, which are aligned with the value we provide.

Remember to always **know, articulate, and protect your value when you are moving through your career and growing as a leader**. It will support your growth, success and increase awareness of the value of those you lead and others in your organization.

How well do you understand and communicate your value to others?

Have you ever felt like your value was not fully appreciated in a job assignment?

What areas of your performance, experience or expertise should be further recognized within your organization?

We each bring value to our workplaces, families, communities and businesses. The hope is that this chapter supports you to further recognize the value you bring each and every day.

Next Steps:

UNLOCKING YOUR LEADERSHIP

Goals for Chapter 6

What goal(s) would you like to set for yourself based on this chapter?

Bernadette Spencer will provide insights on ways to nurture hidden talents of others along your leadership journey in the next chapter.

Author: Kaisha McCrea, MBA

Co-Authors from left to right (Kaisha McCrea, Jana Pollard and Bernadette Spencer)

Chapter 7 -Nurturing Hidden Talent

Measuring Impact: The Return on Investment (ROI) of Nurturing Hidden Talent

"Everything rises and falls on leadership." – *John Maxwell*

Do you remember the first person who believed in you? Who saw something in you that you did not see in yourself?

In the world of business, every leader aims for success, be it in productivity, profitability, or team cohesion. In today's fast-paced world, cultivating a supportive culture that celebrates the discovery of hidden talent isn't just nice to have—it is crucial to fostering innovation and engagement, especially when we focus on nurturing the women-only aspects within the workplace. Often overlooked is a rich source of potential that tends to lie beneath the surface: the hidden talents of team members. Identifying and nurturing this talent can lead to transformational success for the individual, team, and organization. I will share insights to support understanding, identifying and nurturing hidden talent in organizations and teams.

Understanding Hidden Talent

First, let's clarify what we mean by "hidden talent." Hidden talent refers to the skills, abilities, and potential that are not immediately evident in an individual's current role or duties. For instance, a team member may excel in creative problem solving but is currently confined to a repetitive task that does not highlight their capabilities. Similarly, someone may possess leadership qualities but has yet to be given the opportunity to take charge of a project. Misplaced talents can not only hinder team performance but also lead to dissatisfied employees who feel underappreciated.

To effectively nurture hidden talent within your team, consider adopting a structured approach to enable team members to uncover their areas of expertise. Here are strategies that can help leaders identify and foster the potential within their organization:

Step 1: Recognize Barriers to Expression

Start by acknowledging that certain groups, such as women or minorities, may feel less encouraged to share their insights or showcase their skills due to existing stereotypes and biases. This understanding is crucial for creating an inclusive environment where everyone feels valued.

Step 2: Create Development Programs

Initiate targeted development programs that focus on crucial skills like negotiation, public speaking, and executive presence. Tailoring workshops to these areas can empower individuals to step out of their comfort zones and build their confidence.

Step 3: Encourage Collaboration

Foster collaboration among diverse team members. By form-ing groups that include individuals from various backgrounds, you can unlock a wealth of unique perspectives and talents that might otherwise remain hidden. This diversity can enhance creativity and problem-solving.

Step 4: Cultivate a Supportive Community

Encourage team members to share their stories and celebrate one another's achievements. By building a strong sense of community, individuals will feel more inclined to support one another, which can lead to a boost in collective motivation and morale.

Step 5: Recognize Contributions

Create regular opportunities for team members to present their work, regardless of size or scope. This may include monthly meetings where individuals can showcase projects and share successes. For example, highlight a team member who contributed significantly behind the scenes—she may not realize how impactful her work is until it is acknowledged by her peers.

Step 6: Promote Visibility from Leadership

Ensure that senior leaders actively participate in recognizing contributions. This could involve incorporating shout-outs into company newsletters or dedicating time in meetings to celebrate wins. When leadership highlights these successes, it sends a powerful message that every contribution is valuable, fostering a deeper sense of purpose and commitment within the team.

Step 7: Reflect on the Impact

As you cultivate this culture of acknowledgment, observe the ripple effects it creates throughout the organization. Employees will begin to feel that their participation truly matters, inspiring greater loyalty and dedication.

By systematically implementing these steps, you can create an environment where hidden talents are not only recognized but also celebrated, leading to a more engaged and productive workforce.

The Importance of Identification

Identifying hidden talent is the first step in nurturing it. As leaders, we must engage proactively with our team members through ongoing dialogue - the foundation of any successful relationship. By asking open-ended questions about their interests, ambitions, and skills outside their designated roles, leaders can uncover valuable insights. Regular performance reviews are not solely about evaluating past achievements; they should serve as a platform for exploration and discovery.

Identifying Hidden Talents

Next, it is essential to look deeper. Pay close attention to the individuals whose talents may not be immediately visible. For instance, you may have a team member who excels at building client relationships but rarely voices their thoughts in meetings. Instead of overlooking them, take the initiative to engage them in one-on-one conversations. Ask them about their successful strategies and methods. By investing time in these dialogues, you not only uncover hidden skills but also demonstrate that you value their contribution

Leaders play a crucial role in discovering and nurturing the hidden talents of their team members, particularly among underrepresented groups. Outlined below are some strategies leaders can incorporate that can be effective in fostering an environment that encourages individuals to reveal their unique skills and passions.

1. Create Dedicated Initiatives

Establish programs or initiatives that focus specifically on empowering employees. For example, consider launching a women-only group or similar initiative aimed at providing a safe and supportive space for individuals to explore their skills outside their defined job roles.

2. Encourage Skill Sharing

At the beginning of such initiatives, invite participants to share their hidden talents and interests with the group. This can involve activities where team members disclose unexpected skills, such as artistic pursuits or public speaking abilities. Such sharing can inspire others to talk about their own strengths and passions.

3. Revamp Performance Reviews

Transform traditional performance review processes by incorporating discussions that focus on personal aspirations and untapped potential. Introduce components like "Vision Conversations" during reviews to explore each team member's ambitions and hidden talents, rather than solely evaluating past performance.

4. Engage with Thoughtful Questions

During these conversations, leaders should ask open-ended questions that prompt reflection and creativity. Examples include:

- "If you could design your dream project, what would it look like?"

- "What skills are you eager to develop?"

These inquiries can help uncover interests that might not surface in typical job-related discussions.

5. Leverage Unique Skills

Recognize and leverage the unique skills of your team members in practical ways. For instance, if a team member has a background in performing arts, consider how this skill can enhance communication within the team. This could lead to creating workshops that empower others to develop similar communication skills, fostering a culture of growth and confidence.

6. Foster a Culture of Curiosity

Create a workplace environment that values curiosity and exploration. Encourage team members to showcase their talents in team settings and collaborative projects. This will not only enhance team dynamics but also foster creativity and innovation throughout the organization.

Leaders have the power to unlock hidden talents within their teams, and nurturing these abilities leads to a more vibrant and innovative workplace. By engaging with team members beyond their job titles and fostering an open environment, organizations can tap into the unique gifts of their employees, enriching both individual careers and the overall culture. ***Remember, everyone has unique talents waiting to be discovered—it's essential to create the opportunities for them to shine.***

The ROI of Nurturing Talent

There is a compelling return on investment (ROI) in nurturing hidden talents. First and foremost, employees who feel their skills are recognized and developed are more likely to contribute positively to their roles. When a team member is engaged and fulfilled, their productivity can skyrocket. Think about a team where everyone is operating in their area of strength. This alignment leads to more efficient workflows and innovative outcomes.

In addition, nurturing talent can significantly improve employee retention. High turnover rates can be costly – not just financially, but in terms of team morale and cohesion. When employees feel recognized for their unique talents, they are less likely to seek new opportunities elsewhere. Thus, investing time and resources into identifying and developing these strengths leads not just to retained talent but a more committed and motivated workforce.

Creating Development Opportunities

Once you identify hidden talents, the next step is to create practical development opportunities. This might involve offering training, assigning stretch assignments, or pairing individuals with mentors who can foster their growth. Consider establishing a system of micro-mentoring or peer-coaching, where team members can learn from one another in low-pressure environments.

A notable example of nurturing hidden talent among women is the presence of women focused programs, like those offered by organizations such as Deloitte, a global consulting agency. These programs create safe spaces where women can share experiences, build networks, and develop skills specific to their careers in tech and other fields. By focusing on collaboration and empowerment, such initiatives help uncover latent potential, boost confidence, and provide practical strategies for overcoming gender-specific challenges. This supportive environment fosters personal growth and enhances visibility for women, leading to greater opportunities for advancement and innovation. (deloitte.com, careersatdeloitte.com)

"Research findings consistently confirm that those organizations with the most women as senior leaders enjoy rates of return that are greater – often by double-digits – than those with far fewer or no women in their leadership ranks."- Sharon Allen, former Chairman of the Board, Deloitte LLP

(Deloitte.com)

"Our network is important to teach women to get the best out of themselves."-Wilhemina Feenstra -Sponsoring Partner Deloitte Women's Network (deloitte.com)

In the pursuit of gender equality in leadership, many organizations are recognizing the importance of creating spaces specifically for women. These women-focused programs are not just about having a different room for meetings; they are about tailoring experiences that truly address the unique challenges women face in the workplace.

Learning from Other Sectors

Deloitte's initiative is just one piece of a growing tapestry of women-focused programs across various industries. Here are a few noteworthy examples from tech, manufacturing, and education:

1. Google's "#IamRemarkable" Initiative: In the tech sector, Google has launched #IamRemarkable, which empowers women and underrepresented groups to promote their achievements. Special cohorts are created exclusively for women in technical roles—where self-promotion can feel particularly daunting. Workshops help women practice self-advocacy, allowing them to articulate their contributions and step into visible leadership roles. (thinkwithgoogle.com)

2. Caterpillar's "Women in Leadership" Program: Within the heavy machinery and manufacturing industry, Caterpillar delivers leadership training tailored specifically for women in operational and engineering roles. This program connects participants with senior leaders who advocate for their advancement while fostering peer support networks to help diminish the sense of isolation many women face in these male-dominated environments. Caterpillar explains that:

"Our success depends on having the top talent. The increased complexity of our business challenges demands that we have the right talent in the right place at the right time. Research even shows that companies that achieve gender balance, especially at leadership levels, yield more positive results. This issue matters to both men and women and is essential to the fulfillment of our company's values on a global scale. When women play a vital role at Caterpillar, the whole company wins." (caterpillar.com)

3. The "WomenEd" Movement: In the world of education, the WomenEd movement works to increase representation of women in school leadership. Their coaching and mentoring programs provide female educators with the encouragement to pursue senior leadership roles, regardless of non-linear career paths. By focusing on visibility and breaking those self-imposed ceilings, they are uplifting capable women into leadership positions. (womened.com)

As we can see from the success stories of Deloitte and others in different sectors, nurturing hidden talent in women requires more than goodwill; it necessitates thoughtful, targeted approaches that address specific challenges women face in their careers. By creating women-only spaces, organizations can foster an environment where women are not only encouraged to expand their horizons but are truly empowered to fulfill their leadership potential.

Additional workshops or skill-sharing sessions can be tailored to your team's unique talents and interests. For instance, a team member skilled in graphic design might lead a session on visual communication. This not only builds skills within the team but also validates the talents of the individual leading the session, fostering confidence and leadership skills in the process.

In a world where the balance of gender representation in leadership remains skewed, these initiatives provide a blueprint for how to not just level the playing field, but to uplift those who may have felt invisible in their journey. *By shining a light on hidden talent, we can not only foster individual growth but also drive meaningful change across entire industries.*

Building a Supportive Culture

It is essential to cultivate a culture that celebrates the discovery and nurturing of hidden talents. Acknowledgment from leadership can go a long way. Regularly showcase team successes that arise from leveraging hidden abilities, whether in team meetings or company communications. Celebrate both small and large wins that stem from recognizing and utilizing these talents.

How Leaders Can Nurture Hidden Talent

In today's fast-paced world, marked by fierce competition and ever-evolving expectations, it is easy to overlook the hidden gems within our teams. More often than not, the loudest voices in the room command the spotlight, while the quieter, more introspective members may hold incredible potential just beneath the surface. This is particularly true for women in the workplace, whose invaluable contributions can sometimes be overshadowed. As a leader, it is your duty to nurture this talent, ensuring that every individual has the opportunity to shine.

Creating a Welcoming Space

The first step in uncovering hidden talent is to create an environment where everyone feels safe and supported. Picture this: a vibrant workplace buzzing with the energy of diverse voices. To achieve this, consider hosting regular gatherings, like "Women in Sales" lunch-and-learns. These sessions serve as a platform not only for sharing strategies and tips but also for fostering connections among female colleagues. It's about building a community where women feel valued and encouraged, allowing them to share their ideas and experiences openly.

By establishing a warm, welcoming atmosphere, you lay the groundwork for meaningful conversations. Encourage the team to embrace vulnerability, reminding everyone that every story matters and every perspective is valuable.

Encouraging Participation

As these gatherings take shape, it is crucial to cultivate participation. This is where the roundtable format comes into play. Introduce a system that allows each participant the time to speak and share their insights. This approach is particularly beneficial for quieter team members who may feel intimidated in more traditional settings. With everyone getting their turn, you'll notice how the dynamics shift—voices that were previously tucked away start to emerge. You might be surprised by the wealth of ideas and perspectives your team has to offer.

Celebrating Small Wins

Recognizing achievements, no matter how small, plays a pivotal role in nurturing hidden talent. When leaders acknowledge the efforts of their team members, it reinforces the notion that every contribution matters. Share stories of success and highlight the ways in which these efforts positively impact the business. Make it a regular practice to celebrate both individual accomplishments and team milestones. This not only boosts morale but also cultivates an atmosphere of appreciation and motivation—where everyone feels they can make a difference.

Offering Leadership Opportunities

Once you have identified hidden talents, the next step is to empower these individuals by offering them leadership opportunities. Whether it's running a workshop, presenting to the team, or mentoring new hires, give them the chance to take the lead. These roles serve to build confidence and enhance visibility, allowing their talents to flourish in ways they may never have imagined. *Remember, leadership doesn't always come from a title; it can also emerge from having the right platform to express one's skills.*

Fostering Continuous Learning

To truly nurture talent, you must also create an environment that champions growth and development. This might mean offering resources, training, or specific mentorship programs designed to empower women within the organization. By investing in pathways for personal and professional development, you illuminate talents that might have otherwise remained hidden. Encourage your team to pursue new skills and knowledge; as they grow, so too will the organization.

Building a Feedback Culture

Lastly, it's vital to establish a culture where feedback flows both ways. Encourage your team members to share their thoughts on processes and leadership. This open dialogue not only invites diverse perspectives but also helps you understand how to best support your team. Remind everyone that feedback is not a criticism but a vital tool for growth, clarity, and collaboration.

By nurturing an environment that embraces participation, celebrates achievements, and offers opportunities for leadership, you're setting the stage for hidden talents to rise to the forefront. It's about creating a workplace where everyone has the chance to shine. When this happens, incredible outcomes can arise—not just for individuals but for the organization as a whole. Together, let's commit to recognizing and empowering the voices that are ready to be heard, knowing that the sum of our collective talents is far greater than its individual parts.

When team members with various skills and backgrounds work together, they can learn from one another and push each other to excel. This synergy often leads to innovative solutions and stronger team performance. Remember, some of the most remarkable talents often lie just beneath the surface, waiting for the right moment—and the right environment—to shine!

Short-Term vs. Long-Term Gains

The benefits of nurturing hidden talent materialize in both the short and long term. Initially, organizations may notice a boost in team dynamics, communication, and overall morale. Employees who feel that their contributions matter are likely to bring their best selves to work every day.

In the long run, however, the impact can be even more profound. As team members develop their skills and embrace new challenges, they position themselves for advancement, creating a pipeline of capable leaders within the organization. This not only maximizes the potential of your workforce but also equips your organization to respond effectively to future challenges and opportunities.

Leadership's Role

As leaders, you have the unique opportunity to set the tone for how talent is nurtured. Be proactive in seeking out hidden strengths and demonstrating a genuine interest in your team members' growth. Schedule regular check-ins that focus not on performance metrics alone but on individual aspirations and goals.

Balancing the needs of the organization with those of individual team members requires care and intention. Providing feedback that is both constructive and positive encourages a growth mindset and fosters an environment where all team members can thrive.

The Ripple Effect

Beyond the immediate benefits for your team, nurturing hidden talents can create a ripple effect throughout the entire organization. Companies that prioritize talent development see improved customer satisfaction, increased innovation, and enhanced brand reputation. When your team is enthusiastic and skilled, the quality of service or product naturally improves, leading to loyal customers and a stronger market presence.

Conclusion: A Call to Action

Identifying and nurturing the hidden talents of your team members isn't just an exercise in personnel management; it's a strategic business decision with far-reaching implications. As you take steps to uncover these abilities and foster growth, consider the positive outcomes that align with your organization's goals.

By investing in your team's potential, you pave the way for enhanced productivity, stronger retention rates, and long-term organizational success. The benefits extend beyond the immediate gains; nurturing hidden talent can lead to a thriving, innovative culture where everyone is empowered to contribute to the organization's success. Embrace this journey of discovery and watch as your team cultivates the kind of environment conducive to greatness.

Chapter Exercise:

- Engage with your team regularly to identify hidden talents

through open conversations.
- Create development opportunities like training or mentor-ship programs to nurture these skills.
- Foster a supportive culture by celebrating successes that arise from leveraging hidden talents.
- Prioritize individual growth alongside organizational goals to enhance overall team productivity.
- Measuring Impact: The ROI of Nurturing Hidden Talent

Next Steps:

UNLOCKING YOUR LEADERSHIP

Goals for Chapter 7

What goals would you like to set for yourself based on this chapter?

Author: Bernadette Spencer, MEd (Coach & Trainer)

Chapter 8 - Summary & Next Steps

We hope you gained insights from this book to support your leadership growth and success. We encourage you to start where you are today and reduce procrastination on opportunities, address your fears, and recognize and share your leadership experience, potential, and expertise with others.

We hope you are better equipped to trust your decisions, use your power as women leaders, and tap into the power of your network as you continue to move in your career. We encourage you to resist the desire to compare your growth and progress to others as we each have our unique challenges, strengths, and opportunities.

The next few days after you close this book are critical. What steps and goals will you commit to in order to strengthen your leadership skills based on the insights shared in this book?

As a way to support your next steps, enclosed is a link to a template to document and follow your progress over the next 30, 60, and 90 days on the key goals you have identified for your leadership growth and success.

Please see the link below:

www.growingperspecitves.com/resources

If you want to purchase an Unlocking Your Leadership workbook or want to join the Unlocking Your Leadership Coaching group, please email info@growingperspectives.com for more details.

We encourage you to seek help to support your success and celebrate your growth and success.

Stay Connected with Us

You are invited to share your leadership journey updates with us through email (info@growingperspectives.com) and following Growing Perspectives Career Consulting on social media (Facebook, Instagram and LinkedIn) and our website www.growingp erspectives.com. You can also share your comments on which chapter resonated with you the most by emailing us at the email listed above.

You can also reach out to the authors directly:
  Bernadette Spencer: B@bernadettespencer.com
  Jana Pollard: MrsJanaPollard@gmail.com
  Kaisha McCrea: Kaisha @growingperspectives.com

Our desire is that this book helped you realize the need to support and recognize hidden talent within yourself and in your organizations. The opportunity to lead is special and we as women are well equipped to make a lasting impact in any organization.

We hope you have taken the time to complete the questions enclosed to actively reflect on the needed opportunities in your leadership journey to become a more successful leader.

Authors of **Unlocking Your Leadership: Achieve Success and Change Organizations!** (from left-right) Kaisha McCrea, Jana Pollard, Bernadette Spencer

Author: Kaisha McCrea, MBA

Conclusion

Thank you for reading *Unlocking Your Leadership, Achieve Success and Change Organizations!* We are grateful for the opportunity to share practical insights and examples of leadership to support your growth and development. We are excited for you to continue *Unlocking Your Leadership, Achieve Success and Change Organizations!*

Meet our Authors!

Kaisha McCrea, MBA - CEO & Founder of Growing Perspectives Career Consulting. She is an International Coaching Federation certified Career & Leadership Coach, consultant, author, radio personality and speaker. Recognized as a Top 15 Coach in Richmond, Virginia for 2023 by Influence Digest +. Leverages 20+ years of corporate experience in business and community leadership roles. Kaisha is a graduate of North Carolina A&T State University with a BS degree in Chemical Engineering and an MBA from Wilmington University. She is a Core Essentials graduate of Coach U. She resides in Central Virginia with her husband and sons.

Jana Pollard, MBA - An accomplished leader, speaker, and author with a passion for inspiring others to lead with purpose and authenticity. She holds a degree in Mechanical Engineering from North Carolina A&T State University and an MBA from the University of Delaware. As a Regional Operations Leader overseeing North and South America, Jana brings over a decade of experience in engineering and operations management. Jana is also CEO and Chief Solutions Officer of Exclusive Pollard Entity, a solutions-driven company delivering a strong commitment to understanding unique challenges and crafting meaningful solutions. A devoted wife and mother, Jana leads with service, heart, and purpose.

Bernadette Spencer, MEd - Certified Speaker, Coach, and Trainer, and a member of the Maxwell Leadership Certified Team with a certification from the University of South Florida in Diversity, Equity and Inclusion. Specializing in education, success mindset development, leadership empowerment, entrepreneurship, coaching, speaking, and training. She works with leaders, entrepreneurs, organizations and individuals to foster personal, professional, and leadership growth, emphasizing the transformative power of mindset. Bernadette holds degrees in Sociology and a Masters in Education from Virginia Commonwealth University. She co-owns Destiny Designed Unlimited LLC, a consulting agency, with her husband.

We like to thank our families for their support during the writing of this book. We like to thank our mentors, friends, advisors

73

and sponsors over the years who have supported our growth and experiences. We like to thank our editor, Maurice Gray, Jr. for his support. Thanks to Stephanie Garr Photography for capturing our pictures shown through the book. We also like to thank Fred Nash for providing a wonderful book cover that expresses our vision for this topic. And lastly, we want to thank Stan Chambers Jr. of CGSC Creative for editing our book and shooting video highlighting our expertise.

To stay connected with Growing Perspectives Career Consulting please visit our website at www.growingperspectives.com. We are honored to provide this first book from our **Women In Leadership** initiative to support leadership development & success for Women leaders. We are available for speaking, training, consulting and coaching engagements with organizations and individual leaders.

Continue **Unlocking Your Leadership, Achieve Success and Change Organizations!**

Afterword

Unlocking Your Leadership, Achieve Success and Change Organizations! is a wonderful addition to our Women in Leadership initiative provided by Growing Perspectives Career Consulting.

Our organization recently celebrated 5 years of business supporting organizations, individuals, groups and teams! We are grateful that the release of this book aligns with our 5th year of being fully operational. We look forward to continuing to support our clients to grow and thrive as leaders , organizations and through out their careers.

Reaching this milestone of launching *Unlocking Your Leadership, Achieve Success and Change Organizations!* is a wonderful way to continue to support Women leaders to grow and be more successful. Please enjoy a few behind-the-scene moments as we discussed this book.

Bernadette Spencer with our Editor– Stan Chambers, Jr.

We like to thank every client we have served over the past 5 years and every organization that allowed us to provide services to your employees and leaders. It is with the experiences gained over time that propelled us to pursue this book.

Jana Pollard

We anticipate providing additional books in the coming years that will focus on leadership, confidence, business and more! If you like to join our mailing list for updates on future events and books please email us at Info@growingperspectives.com

Kaisha McCrea

Growing Perspectives Career Consulting looks forward to continuing to support our clients to grow and thrive as leaders, organizations and through out their careers. Thank you for purchasing **Unlocking Your Leadership, Achieve Success and Change Organizations!**